WINNING TUBBY

by Lynn Cullen
illustrated by Jacqueline Rogers

MODERN CURRICULUM PRESS
Pearson Learning Group

Liz sat at the kitchen table, chewing the top of her pen. She paid little attention to her parents, who were working on dinner at the stove. She paid even less attention to her brother, who was petting Max, the family cat. Seldom did Liz have business as important as this. She was about to write the most important essay of her life.

If only she knew how to begin.

"Stop doing that, Liz," said her brother, Hank.

Liz looked up with a frown. How was she supposed to write an important essay with her little brother bothering her? "Stop what?"

"Stop chewing on that pen," said Hank, picking up Max. "Do you know how yucky it is to find one of your chewed-up pens in the drawer? You're worse than Ranger."

"Sometimes a person has to chew," said Liz. "Why do you think they invented gum?"

She glanced at her feet where her dog, Ranger, slept. Next to Ranger, she saw one of her father's new running shoes. The sides were riddled with toothmarks, the laces were torn into shreds, and the heel was completely gone.

Ranger had struck again.

Liz glanced at her father, who was stirring the chili on the stove. When Dad found the shoe, he was not going to be happy.

Liz sighed. She had more important things to think about now than a dog with an appetite for shoes.

"Mom?" Liz said.

Her mother got a mixing bowl from the cupboard. "Yes?" she answered.

"I need to write the best essay in the world. How should I start?"

"What's the subject?" asked her mother, cracking an egg into the bowl.

"I want to take Tubby, the class hamster, home over winter break. So does everybody else. So Ms. Quinn said we have to write an essay about why we should be the family that gets him."

"Think of an essay as an argument," said her mother. "You're trying to convince the reader of something. In this case, you're trying to make Ms. Quinn see you're the right one for the hamster."

"But how?"

Her mother got out a bag of cornmeal and measured some into a cup. "Explain exactly how you'll take care of it."

"Everyone knows how to care for a hamster," said Liz. "You give them food pellets once a day and make sure there's water in the bottle."

Hank wrinkled his nose. "What about when its cage gets dirty?"

Liz shrugged. "No big deal. You just clean it."

"Put all that in writing," said Liz's mother, "to show that you know what needs to be done."

Liz's father tasted the chili on his wooden spoon. "If you really want the hamster," he said, "you should take your argument one step further. Don't just explain how to care for the little guy. Prove that you can make its life better."

"How am I going to do that?" Liz exclaimed, flopping back in her chair. Ranger woke and licked Liz's hand.

Hank kissed Max on top of the head. "Why do you even want a hamster? We've already got Max and Ranger."

Liz bit her pen. It was true. She already had plenty of pets. They demanded more care than Liz could give them. How was she supposed to remember to feed and brush them each day? It was all she could do to take care of them, do her homework, and practice soccer kicks in the yard. Good thing her mother never forgot their animals!

Still, Liz thought Tubby was special. He seemed smarter than the average hamster. It fascinated Liz to watch him stand on his haunches like a miniature person to study the world outside his cage. He seemed to know instantly if someone was just staring at him, or if they had food. Tubby loved food.

Tubby proved he was smart in other ways too. If someone accidentally left the top of the cage open a tiny bit, he would wriggle out in an instant. He had fascinated the class by escaping twice already this year. The first time, Ms. Quinn found him asleep in her desk drawer. The second time, a teacher discovered him in a closet two classrooms down the hall.

Any way you looked at it, Tubby was special. He *must* be, Liz figured, the way everyone was fighting to take him home.

After dinner, with her stomach full of cornbread and chili, Liz sat on her bed. She had to be the one to take Tubby home for the holidays. It was time to write the world's best essay.

She thought of her mother's advice. She said Liz should explain how she'd care for the hamster. She began writing.

I should get Tubby over winter break because I will take better care of him than anyone else in the class. I will feed him and check his water twice a day without fail, and I will clean his cage each day.

She pictured Ranger and Max following behind her when she brought Tubby's cage into the house. Ranger would probably like to lick Tubby.

She bent over her paper.

I won't let any other animals near Tubby—not even if they're friendly, and especially if they are not. Tubby will be totally safe.

Liz thought of her father's advice. Now she should tell how she could make Tubby's life better. She chewed on her pen a long time before starting to write again.

Tubby will become a better hamster if he stays with me. I will give him lots of exercise to get him into the best shape of his life. I will even use the experience I have had with other animals to teach him new tricks.

Liz stopped. She wasn't sure if Tubby knew any *old* tricks besides escaping from his cage. In fact, she wasn't sure what tricks she could teach Tubby. She didn't think a hamster could shake hands like Ranger. Seldom would a hamster be interested in rolling over, and there was no way a hamster would fetch.

Liz sighed. Well, she'd train Tubby to do
something . . . somehow.

Now, thought Liz, it's time for a good ending
to the essay. She thought of Hank's comment. Why
did she even want a hamster when she already had
a dog and a cat? Didn't she already have more than
enough to think about?

*I want Tubby because I am naturally good with
animals. My experience in raising cats and dogs has
made me an expert in the field of pet care. I want
Tubby because I would be the best host he could get.*

Liz put down her pen. It was a beautiful essay, full of good strong points. Surely, she'd win the right to take home Tubby. She'd be such a perfect hamster keeper that maybe she could have Tubby over spring break too. Maybe she could even take care of Tubby during the summer. Maybe, just maybe, she could keep him forever!

At the beginning of class the next morning, Ms. Quinn clapped her hands. "Anyone who has brought an essay about taking Tubby home should bring it up now."

Liz hopped out of her seat. She ran to get in line behind the other kids who were putting their essays on Ms. Quinn's desk. She took her place behind Charlotte White, the quietest girl in class.

Liz smiled to herself. Charlotte would never be able to write an essay that would convince Ms. Quinn to let her take Tubby. Charlotte seldom talked at all.

Charlotte laid her essay on the pile. Liz stepped up behind her. She couldn't help but see Charlotte's paper. She smiled to herself. Charlotte's essay was ridiculously short—only two pitiful, little sentences long. Ms. Quinn would never give Tubby to a person who wrote two pitiful, little sentences. Liz leaned forward to read them.

I have no pets. I would like Tubby because I am lonely.

The smile melted from Liz's face.

The rest of the day, Liz watched Charlotte. During the group project for social studies, Charlotte sat quietly by herself.

At lunch, she perched at a table with no company other than her sandwich and an apple.

After lunch, when all the other kids were spilling back into the classroom, talking and laughing, she walked back alone.

Charlotte slipped noiselessly over to Tubby's cage and watched him with a fascinated expression. When she thought no one was looking, she dropped a crust from her sandwich into the cage. He woke from his sleep and gobbled it up as if it were a fine treat.

Liz saw Charlotte's mouth twitch into a smile before it settled back into its normal tight line.

Just before the bell rang at the end of the day, Ms. Quinn made an announcement. "I've received some very nice papers about Tubby today. I didn't realize you were all so fascinated by him. Whenever I look at him, he seems to be sleeping. Well, I promised I'd give him to the person who wrote the best essay. And now we have a winner." She turned to Liz. "Liz, how would you like to take home Tubby?"

Liz glanced at Charlotte just as Charlotte lowered her head.

The bell rang. "Come get Tubby, Liz," said Ms. Quinn.

Liz trudged forward and picked up the hamster cage. Maybe she did have the best essay. It certainly was full of wise points and clever arguments. However, Charlotte had one argument Liz didn't have—she needed a pet. Feeling heavy-hearted, Liz stopped to whisper something to Ms. Quinn. Then she carried Tubby's cage down the hall.

Outside, Charlotte stood in line for her bus. Liz peered into the cage in her arms. Inside, Tubby, like a tiny sailor on rough seas, struggled to stand to inspect his surroundings. Liz had never seen him look cuter.

Still, she knew what she had to do. She clenched her jaw, then marched over to Charlotte.

"Here," she said, offering Charlotte the cage. "I think you should take him."

Charlotte shied away from Liz as if Liz were crazy. "I thought you wanted Tubby."

"I do." Liz frowned. "It's just that I've got too much to do."

Charlotte continued to stare. "So much to do that you can't take care of a hamster?"

Liz combed her brain for the important tasks that would take her away from caring for Tubby. Just then, a pen slipped out of her jacket pocket. Charlotte picked it up. When she touched the mashed-up, chewed end, she made a strange face. And suddenly, Liz knew the answer.

"I've got to train my dog," she said. "He's a terrible chewer. He eats up everything—my dad's shoes, furniture, you name it. He even popped one of my soccer balls. I've got to teach him not to chew things anymore."

Liz felt guilty for not quite telling the truth. But she couldn't take back her words now.

"Are you sure?" Charlotte whispered.

Liz nodded.

Charlotte's smile came slowly at first. Only after a moment did it bloom, like one of those fast-motion films of a flower unfolding its petals.

Now Liz was really sure. She'd never felt so good in her life.

"Please, take him," she said to Charlotte.

Liz traded the hamster cage for her own yucky pen. For a moment, as she watched Charlotte walk up the steps of her bus with Tubby's cage, she felt a twinge of regret. It's not every day you win a contest. In fact, she'd never won a contest before. And now she had given away her prize.

Then she remembered Charlotte's smile, and how she alone had caused it. Maybe making someone happy was another kind of winning.

Liz turned toward home.

Ranger greeted Liz the moment she opened the door.

"Shake," Liz asked.

Ranger held out his paw.

"Roll over," said Liz.

Ranger dropped onto his back, and then wriggling his hips, flipped himself over.

Liz picked up one of Ranger's squeaky toys. "Fetch!" she ordered, throwing it. It landed behind a chair.

Ranger bounded over to the chair. When he returned, something was in his mouth, but it wasn't the squeaky toy. It was one of Mom's high-heeled shoes.

Liz gently wrestled it from Ranger's mouth. "I guess I'm going to be busy after all." She thought of her own chewed pens. Then she patted Ranger on the head. "Don't worry, boy, we're in this together."